Would you Like to Live on a Small Island?

written by Jenny Alexander
illustrated by Debbie Clark

Contents

Ruth and Peter live on a small island.
It has a primary school and a shop.
There is a ferry to the mainland
three times a week. Ruth loves living
there, but Peter doesn't like it at all.
Read their arguments and then
decide – would you like to live on a
small island?

"It's great living on an island because there are lots of places to play. There are sandy beaches and stony coves. Most of the land isn't farmed, so we can go wherever we like. There's hardly any traffic, so our parents don't worry about us going off on our own. We have lots of freedom."

"I think it's boring. What's the point in having lots of freedom when there's no one around and nothing to do? I like traffic. I wish we had a car. I wish I could just get on a bus or train and go places – that would be brilliant."

"But cars, buses and trains cause pollution. Not having any traffic means the environment is cleaner. It's more healthy living on an island. The buildings are clean, the sea is clear, and there's lots of lovely fresh air."

I think you can have too much fresh air! It's a lot more windy on an island. That's why the trees are all bent over. On the mainland, they have trees as tall as houses. There are all different sorts of trees, too.

"I like the fact that we haven't got lots of trees, because trees get in the way of the view. I also like not having too many different types of plants and animals. It means you can easily get to know them all."

But you never get any surprises.
You can never say, "This is a new flower
I've never seen before! This is a new
bird!" I don't like knowing all the plants
and animals because I prefer to have lots
of new things to learn.

On an island, you know everybody. It's horrible because you can't make a mistake or do something bad without everyone knowing about it. If you feel upset or worried, you can't just keep it to yourself.

How's your geography project coming on?

But knowing everyone makes an island a really safe place to live. There's no stranger danger because there aren't any strangers. There's hardly any crime, so we don't have to worry about locking our windows and doors.

> *Another thing I don't like about living on a small island is that there's nothing to do. You can't go to the cinema or have a swim in a swimming pool. You can't go on day trips to theme parks. You can't join clubs and meet new people your own age.*

But that means we make our own entertainment. We have lots of dances and social events. What's more, because there aren't many people, everyone joins in no matter how old or young they are. It's fun going out all together.

MIND YOUR 'EAD

"Living on an island makes going on holiday very difficult and expensive. You always have to start with the ferry crossing. That's no fun for people who get seasick, or don't like going on boats."

“But the sea crossing makes going on holiday more exciting. It feels like a real adventure. Also, there's something very special about coming home to an island. When you see it on the horizon, it looks magical.”

"It's great going to the island school. There are only eleven children, so it feels more like being in a big family than a school. Everyone plays together, and we don't have any problems with bullying."

"But you can't get a decent game of football in a school with only eleven pupils. You can't make a proper team, and even if you could, there aren't any other schools to play against!"

"You can learn really well in a small class. You can go at your own pace, and you never have to struggle to keep up. You don't have to wait for other people to catch up with you in the subjects you're good at, either."

66 *But you don't get a chance to work in groups, and it can get lonely. Also, as you get older you know you will soon have to go to school on the mainland and live away from your family.* 99

66 *Shopping isn't much fun on an island like this because there's only one shop. That means there's not much choice. Sometimes, if the boat can't get across in bad weather, the shop runs out of fresh food.* 99

66 Only having one shop is great because you don't have to waste time looking around, trying to make your mind up. You can get nearly everything you need there, from bread to wellington boots. If you want something the shop hasn't got, you can always order it from a catalogue. 99

Ruth says it's great living on a small island because:

- you have lots of freedom

- the environment is safe and clean

- you can know all the plants and animals

- there isn't any crime

- you can join in with the grown-ups

- the school is small and friendly

- you don't have to waste time shopping.

Peter says it's horrible living on a small island because:

- there isn't enough to do

- there are no cars, buses or trains

- the environment is boring

- there's no privacy

- you can't go on day trips

- the school is too small

- you can't go shopping.

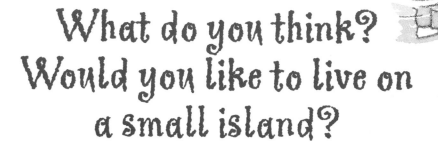

What do you think?
Would you like to live on
a small island?

Index